A Kid's Guide to Flyfishing

A Kid's Guide to Flyfishing

It's More than Catching Fish

Tyler Befus

Johnson Books

Boulder

Published by Johnson Books, a Big Earth Publishing company, 3005 Center Green Drive, Suite 220, Boulder, Colorado 80301. E-mail: books@bigearthpublishing.com www.bigearthpublishing.com 1-800-258-5830

Cover and text design by Constance Bollen, cbgraphics

9   8   7   6   5   4   3   2   1

Library of Congress Cataloging-in-Publication Data is available on file.

Printed in China

Fishing with my family and friends is fun.

I dedicate this book to my Grandpa.

He was so excited for me as I was working on

this project but passed away before it was published.

Thank you for your support Pop. I love you.

Contents

Foreword

In this fun, straightforward guide to flyfishing, Tyler Befus shares his love of flyfishing, and hopes to pass it on to you, too. To understand Tyler better, listen to my flyfishing journey as a young boy. No one understands children flyfishing better than me, because my life in flyfishing started very young.

My fondest flyfishing memories go back to the 1950s when I was a young boy fishing beside my grandfather on the Snake River in front of the Grand Teton Mountain range.

I spent all the summers of my youth with my grandparents until I was seventeen. My grandfather was very English and loved flyfishing. He had learned flyfishing on his first journey to Jackson Hole, Wyoming, in the early 1930s while visiting his cousin who had a dude ranch there. The Snake River ran through her ranch and was home to the native cutthroat trout. His cousin Francis introduced him to Bob Carmichael, lifelong fishing guide and fly-shop owner in the little town of Moose, Wyoming. Moose was the center of my life as I spent all my summers there, along the banks of the Snake River.

My grandfather introduced me to flyfishing at the very young age of five on a guided fishing trip in Yellowstone Park on Lewis Lake. That day I caught my first trout on a fly rod. I remember the fly, a mallard spider, a favorite fly of our mentor, Bob Carmichael. I remember the trip like it was yesterday. The first fish hit my fly and practically pulled the rod out of my hand. The line zipped through the water, going deep into the lake. My grandfather yelled, "Keep the rod high! Reel in the line! Stop! Let him run! Now grandson, reel in more line." The orders flew for quite a while until suddenly the line went slack and my grandfather lifted the net and showed me my first beautiful brown trout. What I remember the most were its colored spots.

Hooked forever on flyfishing, my young mind was consumed by visions of fighting trout. I was blessed to have my grandfather, who would hire a fishing guide twice a week from Carmichael's tackle shop. We would adventure somewhere different each week in the northwest Wyoming area.

Three years later, after many guided fishing trips with my grandfather, I was allowed to go by myself on a small spring creek to discover fishing alone. This trust was my grandfather's second best gift next to the discovery of flyfishing. I loved the quiet I had when I was allowed to fish alone, and it is something I still love today.

My dad and I watching bighorn sheep before fishing the Taylor River.

I had been taught to cast a dry fly and using my grand-father's prized cane rod, I landed my first trout on my own. It was only a seven inch cutthroat trout but it might as well have been a 10 pound trophy.

From then on, flyfishing was everything to me. For Christmas I was given new rods and fly-tying kits. I learned to tie my own flies, and could even sell them and make money! I was allowed to guide fishing trips for adults, and wrote a bestselling book at the age of twenty-four. All of this because I learned to flyfish at a young age—something you can do, too, with the help of this book.

Some people will ask why Tyler would write a book. At such a young age, what would he have to say? How could he know enough? The answer is easy: Tyler loves to flyfish, and wants to share it with other kids. He's written a fun book that will teach you everything you need to know to learn, and love, flyfishing.

Flyfishing isn't for everybody. It is fun, but takes patience and practice. As you read this book, you will learn everything you need to get started as a flyfisher, and hopefully you will love it as much as Tyler and I do.

I believe when you're finished with this book you will become one of us, a flyfisher for life!

Jack Dennis
Jackson Hole, Wyoming

Preface

Hi, my name is Tyler Befus. I'm an average eight-year-old kid who likes to play soccer, football, and basketball and go swimming, but I am totally hooked on flyfishing. I decided to write this book to teach kids about how fun and exciting flyfishing is. I like to flyfish because it is challenging, and I get to learn about many different things: like the different kinds of fish, where fish live, what fish eat, how to use special equipment, and fly casting. I also have been able to learn to tie flies, draw and paint fish, and take pictures of scenery and fish. Along the way I have met very special people who have taught me about flyfishing, fly tying, fish artwork, fly casting, and how to flyfish from a boat while floating a river. Because my whole family likes to flyfish, we get to go to different places all over the country to go flyfishing.

In this book I am going to share some of the basic information you will need to know to start flyfishing. I believe there are not enough young kids that flyfish and I want to change that. I talk to as many kids as I can to try to get them interested in

Casting into a small pond, hoping to catch a big one.

flyfishing. Flyfishing is history, science, art, sport, writing, reading, learning, and teaching others. It sounds like school, but you will find it interesting, challenging, and an exciting adventure that will last your entire life.

Acknowledgments

I would like to thank my dad for teaching my how to flyfish, because if it weren't for him I would not have been able to write this book. I also want to thank my mom because she packs all my snacks and lunches when we go fishing. She also goes fishing with my younger sisters, my dad, and me and never complains. If my mom did not home school me, I would not have the flexible schedule that allowed me to write this book, travel to fish in different places, or do programs for schools and sports shows.

Thanks to expert angler and fly tier Jack Dennis for taking time out of his busy schedule to read the book and write the Foreword for me. Also, a special thanks to Jeff Currier and my art teacher, Mary Hill, for showing me how to draw and paint fish so I could illustrate the book.

Many people have helped me along the way. Mike Bostwick has helped me become a better fly caster, Jon Spiegel at Front Range Anglers taught me about fishing for bass and crappie, and Barry Reynolds taught me about flyfishing for pike before I went to Alaska. Thanks go to Tom Whiting at Whiting Farms,

Dave Heller at Ross Reels, and John Harder and Simon Gawesworth at Rio Products for allowing me to be on their pro staff teams; to Chuck Furimsky and Barry Serviente for inviting me to speak and tie flies at their flyfishing shows around the

Northern Pike

country; to Bruce Olson at Umpqua Feather Merchants for believing in my fly patterns; to Pat and Carol Oglesby for fishing with me and my family and teaching me that flyfishing is about much more than catching fish.

There are so many people who have shown me how to tie flies and provided me with information that there is not enough room to mention them all, but you know who you are. Thank you to all of you.

Catching different kinds of fish is one thing that makes flyfishing so interesting. Here I have a sucker from the Gunnison River.

An Introduction to the Adventure of Flyfishing

What Is Flyfishing?

Before we can answer this question we need to know a few things. First, we need to know what a fly is. We are not talking about a common housefly but a creation of feathers, fur, yarn, thread, beads, and many other things tied on a hook to look like a bug or some other type of food that fish like to eat. Basically, a fly is an imitation of a real bug or other fish food that we use to fool fish.

Fishing is an activity that we do when we are trying to catch a fish. So this would make *flyfishing* an activity that we do to

> *Flyfishing is an activity that we do to catch a fish with an artificial fly.*

catch a fish with an artificial fly. When we are flyfishing, we use a fly rod and fly line to cast an artificial fly and try to make the fly look like a real bug or a real fish swimming in the water so it will fool the fish we are trying to catch.

Now you might ask, what is a fly rod and a fly line? Let me take a minute to explain that to you. A fly rod is a fishing rod that is generally seven to nine feet long and is used with a special reel called a fly reel and a special line called a fly line. A fly reel is much simpler than a casting reel or spinning reel. Most of the time it just holds your fly line, but it does have a braking system called a drag to help with fighting a big fish. The fly line is a special braided line that has a plastic coating to make it slick and adds weight so it can be cast easily with the fly rod. We will learn more about fly rods, fly reels, and fly lines later in the book.

We also need to learn the difference between fly casting and bait casting (also called spin casting). Other types of fishing use weight on the line or a weighted lure or bait to make the line travel out into the water when we cast. Fly casting uses the weight of the special slick fly line to make the cast and deliver our fly to the water. This is called *presenting the fly*, or *presentation of the fly*. The weighted line makes the rod bend while moving the rod back and forth in the air, and this technique is called *loading the rod*. Letting a little bit of the line out with each movement of the rod creates the momentum to deliver the cast. The fly line is a braided line with a slick plastic coating on the outside. Generally there is a tapered leader, which is a single strand of nylon fiber (called monofilament) that is tapered from a thick end to a thin end, attached to the end of the fly line. The leader presents the fly on the water like a real bug.

◉ ◉ ◉

I asked some of my fishing friends for their description of flyfishing. Here are some of their answers:

- "The art of fooling fish while having fun." *Jon Spiegel, Boulder, Colorado*
- "Fly fishing is freedom; freedom to explore the world and experience nature." *David S. Heller, Denver, Colorado*
- "Flyfishing is trying to catch a fish with an imitation of an insect, an imitation that we have made ourselves." *Martin Westbeek, Oisterwijk, Holland*
- "Flyfishing is just a good reason to get out and enjoy nature. It brings you in contact with the river, fish, insect life,

weather, and the environment in general—causing you to focus on all of these instead of yourself." *Tom Whiting, Delta, Colorado*

⊙ ⊙ ⊙

I believe flyfishing is an adventure that includes spending time outdoors learning about nature with family and friends, and it is sometimes about catching fish. Flyfishing is a sport and art form that uses a rod and line to cast a fly to a fish and trick the fish into eating that fly.

Tyler holding one of his first trout caught on the fly rod.

There is not a right or wrong answer to the question, what is flyfishing? Different people fish for different reasons, and there are different parts of flyfishing that people find more interesting than others.

Flyfishing has been a way of life for me and my family for as long as I can remember. I began flyfishing at the age of three. I have actually been flyfishing with my mom and dad since I was old enough to sit in a baby backpack. I would try to cast and hook fish from the backpack—

If you like adventures, then you will love flyfishing.

Tyler watching and learning from the baby backpack.

well actually, my dad would hook the fish and then let me fight them and try to land them while I was in the backpack.

There is much more to flyfishing than the equipment and the fish. When you are a flyfisher you learn about bugs, the outdoors, fish, understanding the currents in a river, fly tying, fly casting, photography, art, wildlife, and traveling to different places. If you like adventures, then you will love flyfishing.

Let me tell you about just one of my flyfishing trips. I was six years old at the time, and it was the middle of winter when my dad asked me if I wanted to go to Alaska the next summer

Tyler and the float plane in Alaska.

to fish for northern
pike and sheefish (some fish have
some very strange and funny names
as we will see later in
the book). I was excited,
happy, and even a little scared all at once.

First, we tied about a gazillion flies, and then we
made sure we had all of our gear and clothing ready for a whole
week of fishing. That was sure a lot of work. After months of
waiting and preparing, June finally arrived, and it was time to
get on an airplane and head north to Alaska. We had to fly on
four different airplanes to get where we were going to fish. The
last one was a floatplane. A floatplane takes off and lands on
water! That was really cool.

We stayed at my Uncle Greg's lodge, which is a 67-foot-
long houseboat on the Innoko River. My good friend Pat
Oglesby went with us, and my Aunt Laurie and cousins Jacob
and Travis were there too. I met some new friends as soon as we
got to the houseboat. They were the other fishing guides, Jason
and Ross. After getting all our rods ready and dressed in our
waders, it was time to go fishing.

We fished from a small boat that our fishing guide Ross
used to take us to different fishing spots. He even let me drive

The houseboat on the Innoko River and my new friends.

First pike on a fly!

the boat with his help. I also made sure to wear my life jacket to make certain I would be safe. Ross took me to a special spot where I caught my very first northern pike. It was 20 inches long and had razor-sharp teeth. My dad took pictures of me and the fish and then we released it back into the water.

A PAGE FROM TYLER'S TRIP JOURNAL

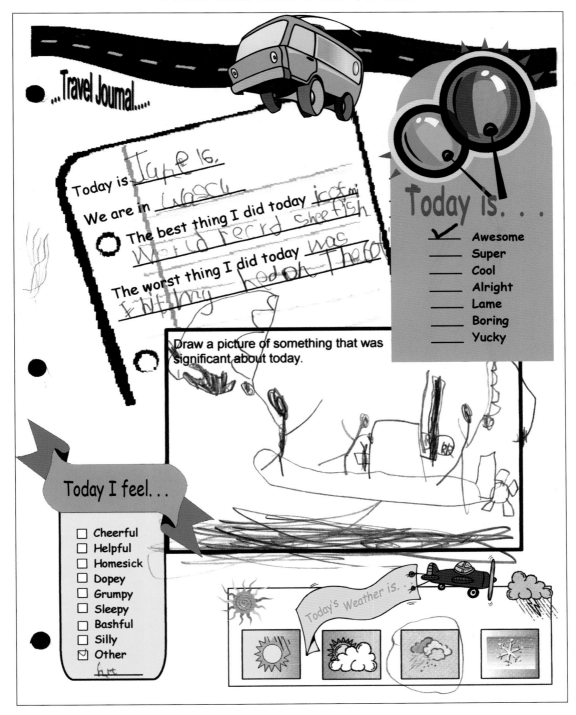

Tyler and his world-record sheefish, caught on the Innoko River.

During the week, I got to fly in the floatplane with my dad and our pilot, Ron, to other places to fish. Ron said I was his youngest passenger ever. When we were flying, we saw moose and bears on the ground below us. I got to eat Eskimo ice cream that is made from mashed up whitefish, blueberries, and Crisco. Yuck! It did not taste very good at all. Each morning before going fishing I would take time to write in my trip journal, which my mom put together for me, about my experiences from the day before so I would always remember my trip there.

Some days we would fish very late, even as late as one o'clock in the morning! It barely gets dark in Alaska during June so it was easy to lose track of what time of day it was. The weather changed constantly. It was sunny, then cloudy, then rainy. The wind would blow, and then the sun would come back out. We caught fish every day, and my biggest pike was 33 inches, which I caught on a fly I tied myself. The last day we fished, it was raining and pretty cold. Then a rainbow appeared, and I found my pot of gold underneath it. I caught a seven-pound sheefish, which is the International Gamefish Association (IGFA) junior angler world record.

Wow, that was a trip I will never forget. It was a true adventure—just like every other day I go fishing. A flyfishing adventure can be just a couple of hours at a local pond catching bluegill, a full day on a river fishing for trout, or even a weeklong trip to Alaska or somewhere else in the world. To start your adventure in flyfishing, turn the page and come with me now to learn about this amazing activity.

Flyfishing is a great way to spend time with your family, enjoying the outdoors. Here I am helping my mom wade across the Gunnison River!

The Fish

2

Fish are a very important part of flyfishing because without them, we would not be able to fish at all. Fish come in all sizes and shapes, from big fish like marlin and sharks to small fish like bluegill and sunfish. Pike and musky are long fish with lots of sharp teeth. Trout have very bright colors. Sailfish are one of the fastest fish on the planet; they can swim up to 68 miles per hour! That is faster than the speed limit on most highways!

Fish come in all sizes and shapes.

LEFT: **Northern Pike** RIGHT: **Rainbow Trout**
BELOW: **Sailfish**

Some fish live in freshwater, and some live in saltwater. Some types of salmon live in both freshwater and saltwater. Just about anywhere you go in the world, it is possible to find fish. And, it is possible to catch almost every kind of fish with artificial flies. Fish like trout, salmon, bass, and panfish are some of

the most popular fish to fish for with a fly rod. Old fishing books tell us that flyfishermen have been flyfishing for trout and salmon for hundreds of years. But, as flyfishing has become more popular and more people are doing it, lots of other fish are now fished for. Saltwater fish like tarpon, bonefish, tuna, and barracuda are among some of the favorites. Even fish like carp, which can grow very large and are often thought of as a yucky fish, are a blast to catch with a fly rod.

TOP: **Kokanee Salmon**

MIDDLE: **Tarpon**

RIGHT: **Carp**

> *Most fish like to live by some kind of structure.*

Learning About Fish

Fish need certain things to survive. They need water, food, and places to hide for protection. Most fish like to live by some kind of structure. Structure can be natural things like rocks, weed beds in the water, a floating log, or an undercut bank. A tree overhanging the water, or even clouds in the sky, which reduce the amount of light on the water, can be considered cover that fish like. Man-made structure can include things like a dock, a

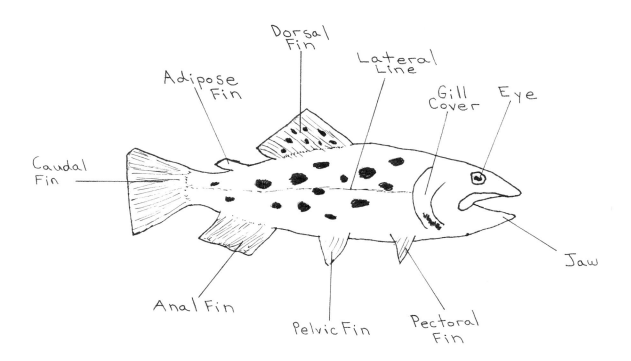

LEFT: **Crappie**
ABOVE: **Bluegill**

shipwreck in the ocean, or big pieces of concrete used to reinforce a bank in a river.

It is also fun to learn the names of different parts of a fish. The drawing to the left shows the different parts that make up a fish.

Most beginning flyfishers learn to fish for panfish, bass, or trout because they are some of the most readily available fish to catch. So let's learn a little more about each one of these fish.

Panfish

This is a common term to describe a group of fish that live in freshwater and include bluegill, crappie, yellow perch, and different types of sunfishes. They are found all over the United States from city park lakes to thousands of farm ponds. They are a great fish to learn to flyfish on because they are easy to find, eat flies really well, and do not require a perfect cast to fool them. Even though they usually do not grow very large, they can really pull hard and give a good fight.

Most panfish spend much of their time in pretty shallow water and many times you can see the fish you are casting your

Tips for Handling Fish When You Are Going to Release Them

- Always try to land them quickly so they do not get too tired out.
- Try to use a net when possible to help land the fish.
- Wet your hands before touching the fish so you do not rub off their protective slimy coating.
- Never squeeze a fish.
- Try to keep them in the water when you remove the hook (using barbless hooks or a hook with the barb pinched down will make it easier to remove the hook).
- Do not keep them out of the water for too long if you want to take a picture of them (they cannot breathe out of the water).
- Make sure the fish is strong enough to swim away before releasing it.

fly to. That is called *sight fishing*. Panfish really spend a lot of time around structure. They use the structure to hide themselves so they can eat bugs and small fish that might swim by. This makes flyfishing for them really neat because you can see them eat your fly if the water is clear.

Panfish are also a good fish to practice your fish handling skills and hook removal skills on because they are pretty tough fish. It is important to treat all fish with respect when handling them. If you are going to release the fish you catch, this is especially true.

Remember, if you kill the fish you will never be able to have the fun of catching that fish again.

Bass

Bass are larger members of the panfish family and also live in freshwater streams and lakes. Some of the most popular bass include smallmouth bass, largemouth bass, and spotted bass. They are also very aggressive toward our artificial flies, making them a good fish to learn or practice flyfishing. Bass can grow very large in the right conditions, giving the flyfisher a chance at catching a really big fish.

They will feed on smaller fish, crayfish, and bugs that live in the water. Many bass flies such as poppers and streamers

Largemouth Bass caught at night on a popper.

look like a small fish or leeches, and they are very cool. Poppers are flies made out of cork, foam, or deer hair that float and make a "popping" or "gurgling" sound when the line is pulled and the fly moves on the surface of the water.

Bass like to spend time around structures to ambush other fish, frogs, crayfish, and bugs just like the panfish. They like to feed at night and fishing with poppers after dark is just one more adventure you can have when flyfishing. When you bass fish at night you will sometimes hear coyotes howling and maybe see some bats flying around in the air.

Trout

There are four basic kinds of trout: rainbow trout, brown trout, cutthroat trout, and brook trout. Trout live in cool or cold freshwater lakes, ponds, streams, and rivers. They eat a lot of insects that live in the water, like mayflies, caddisflies, midges, and stoneflies (we will learn more about these bugs later in the book). They also like to eat small fish or minnows, leeches, crayfish, freshwater shrimp, and aquatic worms. Many insects that live on land are also favorite foods of the trout. These include ants, beetles, grasshoppers, and crickets.

In lakes, trout live by different types of structure and will cruise around looking for food. In streams and rivers, trout mostly stay in one area and wait for the current in the water to bring food to them.

When I was just two years old I caught my first bluegill on a fly rod. It was at a small lake named Chipeta Lake in Montrose, Colorado. Well, I did not catch

There are four basic kinds of trout: rainbow trout, brown trout, cutthroat trout, and brook trout.

The four basic kinds of trout

▲ Brook

Brown ▼

▲ Cutthroat

Rainbow ▼

ABOVE: **Brown Trout**
RIGHT: **Rainbow Trout**

BELOW RIGHT: **Brook Trout**
BELOW LEFT: **Cutthroat Trout**

it completely by myself; I did have help from my mom and dad. Anyway, that little bluegill is the reason I kept on flyfishing and love this activity so much.

Tyler with his first bluegill at Chipeta Lake.

Now, one of my favorite fish to fish for is green sunfish. There is a lake about 20 miles from my house that has some very big green sunfish in it. During the summer, my family and I go fishing there a couple times a week. My five-year-old sister, Ava, has learned to catch green sunfish almost as well as I can. Some evenings we catch as many as 40 or 50 of them in just a few hours when the fishing is red hot. I tied my own special green sunfish fly called the "Secret Weapon." This fly catches all kinds of different fish. I have caught yellow perch, bass, bluegill, carp, trout, and of course green sunfish on it. We will talk about tying your own flies later in the book.

TOP: The "Secret Weapon" fly pattern.
LEFT: Green Sunfish from a small lake near Tyler's house.

Carp are one of the biggest fish you can catch in fresh water with a fly rod.

3

Hey Fish, Where Are You?

There is a little more we need to understand about fish before we start flyfishing. Fish have certain places they like to live and feed, in lakes and in streams. If we know what places these are, it will be a lot easier to catch them.

Understanding the Places Fish Live in Rivers and Streams

Remember from the last chapter that fish like to live around structure. Rivers and streams usually have many different types of structure. Different types of water currents create different types of structure where fish feel safe or can find food. Bugs that are living in the rocks and gravel on the bottom get washed away by the current, and the fish eat them when they float down.

If we understand what these currents do, we can use these currents to know where the fish are. This is called *reading the water*. It is sort of like reading a map. There are many different types of currents in a river or stream. The list below names and describes the most common currents and water types to find fish in a river or stream.

◉ ◉ ◉

Riffle: A riffle is usually a shallow area that has faster moving water flowing over the rocks on the bottom. This makes the water look choppy on the surface. Riffles are also bug factories because the faster current keeps more oxygen in the water. Trout use riffles to feed in during the summer when there is enough water to give them some protection. During the winter, when water levels are lower you will usually not find trout in riffles.

Run: A run is a deeper water section with some larger rocks. Runs can be fast or slow and are a good place for the fish to find protection because the water is deeper and the surface is choppy. This makes it harder for predators to see them in the water. Trout will use runs to feed in all year long as well as a place of safety.

A typical riffle in a river or stream.

A typical run in a river or stream. Fish stay in runs to feed and to hide from predators.

Pool: A pool is an area of deeper water that has slow moving current. Sometimes

A typical pool in a river or stream. Pools provide protection and a place for fish to live when the water is very low, like in winter.

there are larger rocks in a pool that provide structure for the fish. When water levels are lower in the riffles or a shallow run, trout will use pools as their home. Trout will also feed in pools all year long just like in a run.

Pocket water: Pocket water is an area that has rocks sticking

Pocket water in a river or stream. Fishing pocket water is very exciting and fun because the fish can be anywhere. You never know when you will get a strike!

Tyler watching his strike indicator as his nymph drifts in the current seam. Remember, fish like current seams because there is a lot of food drifting down in them for the fish to eat.

out of the water in the current, which creates small areas of slower water behind them. These are called pockets. These pockets are good places for trout to sit and wait for food to come drifting by so they can eat it. Pocket water can be in a riffle, run, or pool.

Current seams are places where fast water and slow water come together.

Current seams: Current seams are places where fast water and slow water come together. Current seams are

A typical eddy.

found in both shallow and deep water in a river or stream. Usually in the faster water there will be a lot of food. The trout can sit in the slower water and eat the bugs as they float by in the current. In pocket water there are current seams created by the rocks sticking up above the surface. Current seams are my favorite type of water to flyfish for trout because I catch a lot of trout in them.

Eddy: An eddy is a current that spins around in a circle. It is created by different speeds of water coming together, usually in a spot where the river turns or has a corner. Eddies create spots that collect a lot of the bugs floating down the river. This makes them a favorite spot for fish to hang out and eat.

Understanding the Places Fish Live in Lakes and Ponds

Since lakes generally do not have moving water, the fish have to move around and search for their food. It is important for us to know where the bugs and small minnows, or baitfish, live so we can find where the trout and bass will be when fishing a lake or pond. There are some things we can look at to understand, or read, a lake or pond just like we do a river or stream.

Since lakes generally do not have moving water, the fish have to move around and search for their food.

⊙ ⊙ ⊙

Inlets: An inlet is the place where a stream or river flows into a lake. Fish like inlets because many food items are washed into the lake by the moving water of the river or stream coming into it. Lakes can have one inlet or a bunch of them.

Weed beds: Weed beds are found in shallow water and deep water. These are places that plants grow in the water. They make homes for the bugs and minnows that live in a lake. They also provide structure for trout, bluegill, bass, and the other gamefish (According to *McClane's New Standard Fishing Encyclopedia*, "A Gamefish is defined as any type of fish that can be taken by sporting methods") that we are trying to catch.

Ledges or drop-offs: Ledges and drop-offs are places where the shoreline or rocks or other structure create a shelf, like in your closet. There can be a flat spot and then the bottom of the lake just drops off into deeper water. These are places that trout and bass will launch a surprise attack on small fish or minnows that swim off the shelf and into the deeper water. Sometimes these drop-offs create a water temperature change in a lake. All fish living in lakes have a water temperature that they are most comfortable living in. Maybe in the summer, when the shallow water becomes too warm for them, they will move to the first drop-off where they will be more comfortable in the cooler temperature.

Points: A point is a piece of land that goes out into the water from the bank or shoreline. A point can be underwater too. This makes a high spot that the fish will use as structure. Sometimes there can be drop-offs or ledges created by a point.

Smaller fish will use a point as a safe place from the deep water. This will cause the big fish to come look for a meal. If a point is rocky, it is a good place for crayfish to live, and this also makes the big fish come to feed because trout and bass really like to eat crayfish.

An inlet to a lake.

A lake with a lot of weed beds for the fish to feed and hide in.

A ledge or drop-off.

A point on a lake.

Steep shorelines: If you look at the land around a lake you can learn a lot about what is under the water. If there is a steep rocky bank right to the edge of the water, it is usually going to make a steep drop-off under the water. If the shoreline is flat or has a gradual slope to the shoreline, it is most likely pretty

A steep shoreline along the dam of a lake.

Tyler casting into a lake from a dam with a steep shoreline.

Tyler fishing one of his favorite spots on the Gunnison River in Colorado. Remember, flyfishing is about having your favorite spots to fish.

shallow some distance from the bank out into the lake. A steep shoreline can be a spot that fish like trout, bass, and panfish like to be because there is deep water close by for them to hide, and sometimes these shorelines will have food items stacked up on them. If the wind is blowing against that steep shoreline, it will push bugs

like ants, beetles, and grasshoppers against it and the fish will come there to eat them.

Man-made lakes and ponds have dams that hold the water back. Sometimes these dams have rocks or concrete along them, which creates structure for the fish. These are also steep shoreline areas that are good to fish.

⊙ ⊙ ⊙

I fish at a ranch here in Colorado that has several small lakes. Some of these lakes have very large trout in them. I have my best success fishing from the dams. It seems like the trout spend their time cruising close to the dam looking for food. So I cast flies that look like small fish and leeches, and the big trout slam them. One day I caught seven trout that weighed over 5 pounds (the biggest one was 8 pounds!) from one of the small lakes using this technique. It makes sense because if a really big trout saw a small fish swimming in the deep water that is out from the dam, the small fish would make an easy meal for that trout.

When I fish the Gunnison River in Colorado, I like to fish the current seams because the fish will sit there waiting for the food to drift down. When they see something they like, they will grab it, and hopefully the thing they grab will be my fly.

All geared up to fish with my mom, dad, and two sisters.

The Gear

Gathering my flyfishing gear has been almost as much fun as the fishing itself. My first fly rod was an ice fishing rod that we put a fly reel and fly line on for me to start casting with. It worked great because it was short and very lightweight for my young arms to handle. A trip to the local discount store with my dad produced a pair of knee-high rubber boots. Yes, my first pair of waders, and I had only been walking for a year and a half! I should mention that all anglers, young

> All anglers, young and old, need to be very careful when wading in the water.

and old, need to be very careful when wading in the water. Our family rule has been that we never get into the water unless a parent is with us and stays within arm's reach.

There are a few basic pieces of gear that you must have to start flyfishing, but it is not necessary to spend a lot of money getting started. In addition to the necessities, there are other pieces of gear that will make your flyfishing experience more enjoyable. Some of the pieces of gear have very funny names.

The following list of equipment shows necessary items to get started and another list of items that are just nice to have to make life easier when you are fishing. I have included a description of each of these different items so you will know what I am talking about later in the book. Some of these items are things that your mom and dad will be responsible for getting together for you before getting out on the water.

Must-Have List

These are items that are essential to start flyfishing.

Fly rod. A fly rod is usually longer than a spinning rod or a casting rod (about seven to nine feet long). But not always. Fly rods come in all different line sizes. For example, a four-weight or five-weight rod is a good line size to start with.

Fly reel. A fly reel holds the line and backing. (Backing is a braided line that goes on your reel before the fly line. It is a filler for the reel and gives you extra line if a big fish takes out all the fly line.) They also come is different sizes just like fly rods. The reel is used to help land fish because you reel them in by cranking the reel. Generally fly reels have an adjustable drag to help you land a big fish. If you are going to fish for really big fish a fly reel with a good drag is impor-tant. The drag of the reel makes it harder

A fly reel holds the line and backing.

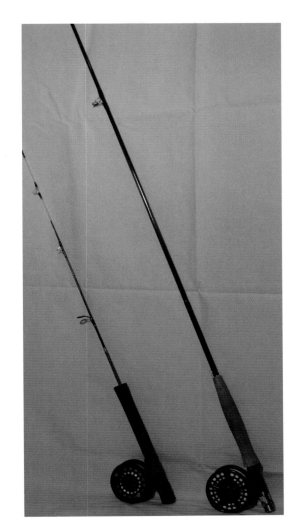

A standard fly rod.
Tyler's first fly rod was an ice fishing rod with a fly reel and line.

A standard fly reel.

A floating fly line and
sinking fly line.

for the fish to pull line off the reel. This makes the fish tired and makes it easier to land the really big fish.

Fly line. The fly line has a braided inside with a slick plastic coating. Some fly lines are made to float and some are made to sink. Fly line is different from regular fishing line because it is bigger around and is weighted. Remember it is the weight of the line that bends, or *loads*, the rod when you are casting. Fly lines come in many different colors. Some are very bright and some are dark. I like brightly colored lines because they are easier to see. Your fly line should match the line weight of your rod. (If you have a four-weight rod, you should use a four-weight fly line to make the rod cast properly.) If the fly line is too heavy or too light for your rod, it makes it hard to cast.

A variety of different tapered leaders and tippet material on spools.

Tapered leader. A tapered leader is tied to the end of your fly line and is made out of monofilament (basically it is fishing line but it is tapered from thick to thin). The last part of the leader is called the tippet. The tippet is not tapered and it is where you tie on your fly. When the tippet is broken or used up from tying knots while changing flies it can be replaced with a new tippet. We will be learning the basic knots later in this chapter. The leader is clear so the fish do not see it when we are trying to fool them with our fly.

Dry flies, wet flies, nymphs, and streamers.

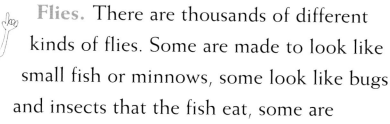

There are thousands of different kinds of flies.

Flies. There are thousands of different kinds of flies. Some are made to look like small fish or minnows, some look like bugs and insects that the fish eat, some are bright, some are dark, some are flashy, some are very small, and some are very big. There are flies that float and flies that sink. The most basic types of flies are dry flies, wet flies, nymphs, and streamers. I will describe what each of these different fly

types are in chapter 6.
Without flies we would not
be able to flyfish!

Hat or baseball cap. A hat
is important to protect us
from the sun and to protect
us from hooking ourselves
when we cast.

**A baseball cap and
a hat with a full brim.**

Polarized sunglasses.
Polarized sunglasses help you
see your fly and help you see
fish because they remove the
glare that the sun makes on
the water's surface. If you do
not have polarized
sunglasses, it's
OK but it is still
very important
to wear
what
you

*Another family
rule is that we can
never ever cast
unless we have on
our sunglasses.*

Polarized sunglasses with a lanyard to keep them around your neck so you do not lose them.

have to protect your eyes from the bright sun and from being hooked in the eye when casting. Another family rule is that we can never ever cast unless we have on our sunglasses.

Sunscreen and insect repellent. It is very easy to get sunburned when you are by the water fishing all day. So it is important to use your sunscreen. Insect repellent is good to have with you so if the mosquitoes start to bite, you can put it on and still enjoy your flyfishing trip. Since some insect repellents have some bad chemicals in them, we only apply this to our hat and clothing to keep the bugs away. Wearing a long-sleeved shirt helps protect you from the sun and from the bugs.

Fishing license. In some places a fishing license is required for kids. It is important to have your parents check the rules and laws in your area before you go fishing. Here in Colorado you do not need to have a fishing license until you are fifteen years old.

Nice-to-Have List

These items will help make your flyfishing experience more enjoyable.

Sunscreen and insect repellent.

Split shot. Small lead or tin weights used on the leader to help sink flies.

Fly floatant. Most fly floatant is like a paste that you put on flies to help them float on the surface and to help keep them dry.

Strike indicator. This is a fancy word for a bobber! Strike indicators come in all different sizes, colors, and shapes. They go on your leader to help you know when a fish eats your wet fly or nymph. We will learn more about these later in the book.

Fly box. A fly box is a box used to store your flies when you are fishing. Some fly boxes have foam to stick the flies into and

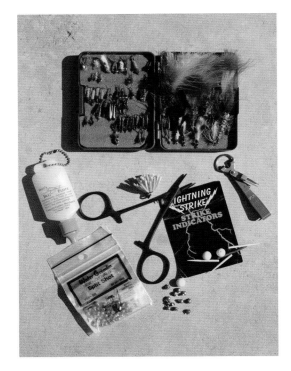

LEFT: Waders, landing net, hat, sunglasses, fly box, and vest.

RIGHT: Flies, split shot, strike indicators, fly floatant, line clippers, and forceps.

some have compartments to store flies. Basically, any small plastic box will work as a fly box.

Waders. Waders keep you dry and warm when you are standing in the water flyfishing. (You can wet wade in shorts and a pair of old shoes during the summer, but it is nice to stay dry with waders, especially when it is cold.)

Long-sleeved shirt. Sleeves protect your arms from sunburn and from mosquito bites.

Rain jacket. Just in case it rains when you are on one of your big adventures.

Line clippers. These are a small clipper like a fingernail clipper to trim line when tying knots. These clippers are much safer than scissors or a pocket knife.

Hemostats/Forceps. This is another special item for flyfishers to help remove flies from the fish's mouth. You can use them to pinch split shot onto your leader and to bend down the barbs on your hooks to make them easier to remove from the fish.

Disposable waterproof camera. It is fun to take a picture of the big one that did not get away to show your friends and family.

Landing net. This makes it easier to land your fish.

Helping my sister Ava hold a nice Brown Trout for a photograph.

The Methods

In this section of the book we are going to talk about different methods or techniques used to catch fish when flyfishing. There are lots and lots of different methods to use in different situations when you are flyfishing. First we should learn some basic casting information so we can understand the different techniques.

Casting Methods

Fly casting is one of the most important things in the sport of flyfishing. If you do not practice casting, you will have a hard

You must practice to become a good fly caster just like playing a sport requires practice.

time catching fish because you must cast your fly onto the water in order to be successful. When you cast your fly, it is important to have good control of your line, leader, and fly. This will help with casting accuracy so you are able to cast the fly where you want it to go on the water. The first type of cast we will learn is an overhead cast. The overhead cast is the most basic cast. Once you learn how to make an overhead cast, you can learn other more difficult casts like curve casts, reach casts, and s-casts. It is always best to practice your casting on the water, but you can also practice on the grass at the park or in your yard. I recommend taking a casting class from an instructor in your area or through a local fly shop. Practice your casting. You must practice to become a good fly caster just like playing a sport requires practice.

Overhead Cast

To start practicing the overhead cast, you need to first become friends with your rod. You should hold the grip of the rod in a way that is comfortable for you. You do not need to squeeze the grip so tight that your hand feels like it will fall off. Remember this is supposed to be fun. I like to think of the rod grip as a hammer when I hold it in my hand. This is a comfortable way for me to hold it. You may find something works better for you. We will start this casting lesson with a short amount of line on the ground in front of us (maybe 10 to 15 feet).

This is how Tyler grips the rod.

It is important to have a leader tied onto the end of your fly line and a small piece of yarn tied to the end of your leader. This will help your cast unroll more easily than if you practice with only the fly line.

There is an easy way to understand the places we stop the rod when we are casting in order to make good casts. If you imagine the numbers of a clock are around you with twelve o'clock being straight above your head (as in the diagrams), this will help you understand the instructions to learn casting.

⊙ ⊙ ⊙

• Step 1: Begin with the rod tip down low so it is close to the water or the grass. Then lift the rod tip up, starting slowly and then going faster. The fly line in front of you will follow the rod, moving up into the air. The weight of the fly line will start to bend the rod. This is called *loading the rod.*

Overhead Cast Diagram #1

• Step 2: Keep lifting the rod until the tip is slightly behind you and then stop moving the rod (stopping the rod tip at about ten o'clock). When you stop the rod, this will form a loop in the fly line as it unrolls off the tip of the rod and is called the *back cast.*

Overhead Cast Diagram #2

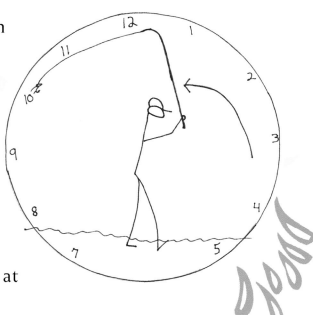

• Step 3: Wait just a moment to allow the loop to straighten out behind you (remember to keep the rod tip at

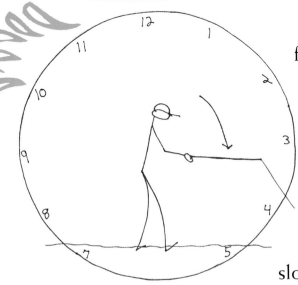

Overhead Cast Diagram #3

Overhead Cast Diagram #4

about ten o'clock when you are waiting). Make sure you do not wait too long or the line will start to fall onto the ground behind you. Once the loop completely rolls out, then you can start to move your arm forward and stop the rod tip just slightly in front of you. The weight of the line will bend, or load, the rod. When you stop the rod in front of you (stop the tip of the rod at about two o'clock), it will form a loop. This called the *forward cast*.

• Step 4: When the line is completely straightened out in front of you, then you can start dropping your rod tip slowly as the line falls back to the water to complete the cast and deliver the fly onto the water (or grass).

⊙ ⊙ ⊙

Let's say you were using an overhead cast to cast your fly behind a rock in a stream and you want to make some casts to a different location. You can use false casts to change the direction of your cast. False casting is when you keep the fly line in the air without letting it touch the ground or the water. So, you keep moving the rod between ten o'clock and two o'clock while you move the direction of your cast toward the direction of your next target.

Fly casting is almost as much fun as fishing.

Fly casting is almost as much fun as fishing. To become good at fly casting, it is very important to practice your casting as much as possible. The better you become at casting, the more fish you will catch when you are out fishing, and the more fun you will have when you can place your fly right where you want it to be.

Here is a fun game to play: Pick a place in your yard or on the grass at the park where you like to stand when practicing your casting. Then put paper plates or pots and pans from your mom's kitchen at different places in front of the place you will be standing. Place some to your right, some to your left, some close to you, and some farther away from you. Then try to cast your piece of yarn onto the plates or into the pots and pans. This is a fun way to test your skills. You can take turns with friends and even keep score to see who can place their fly in the right spot.

Sometimes it is not possible to make a back cast because there will be bushes, trees, rocks, and other things behind you that you will hit or tangle in. If it is low bushes or a low bank on a river, you must stop your back cast higher in the air to keep your line above them. When you cannot use a back cast, there is another useful cast we should learn. It is called the roll cast. The roll cast must be practiced on water because the water actually helps load the rod when making the cast. Let me help you learn how to make a roll cast.

Roll Cast Diagram #1

Roll Cast

• **Step 1:** Hold your rod grip the same way you did for the overhead cast and start with about 15 to 20 feet of fly line on the water and your rod tip down close the water.

• **Step 2:** Slowly lift your rod tip up and back without making the fly line leave the water. Lift the rod tip until the tip is at about ten o'clock behind you and allow the loop of fly line to come up beside your casting arm.

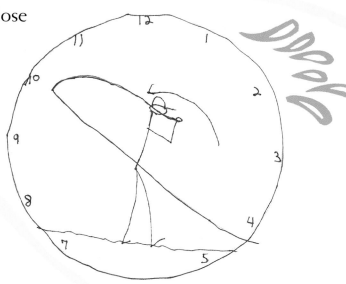

Roll Cast Diagram #2

Roll Cast Diagram #3

• **Step 3:** Once the loop of line stops moving beside you, then you move your arm forward and down (it is kind of like hitting a nail with a hammer) with some power and quickness. The water keeps resistance on the fly line, and this is what bends, or loads, the rod to make the power of the cast. Make sure to

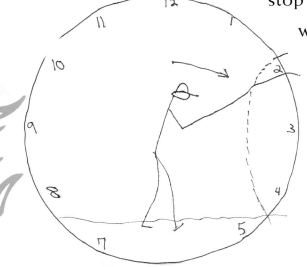

Roll Cast Diagram #4

stop the rod tip before it hits the water (stop the rod tip at about three or four o'clock) when making the forward cast with the roll cast method. If it does hit the water, you know you went too far down with the rod tip. When the rod tip stops, it will cause the line to unroll on the water in front of you. That is the roll cast.

The roll cast is a very useful cast when fishing in small streams that do not have much room for an overhead cast.

The roll cast is a very useful cast when fishing in small streams.

Tying Knots

Before we start to learn more about techniques, we need to learn how to tie a couple of important knots so that we can tie a tippet on our leader and tie flies onto our tippet. The first knot we will learn is called the Double Surgeon's Knot. You can use this knot to tie the tippet onto your leader.

◉ ◉ ◉

• **Step 1:** Place the leader and tippet side by side so they are overlapping about 6 inches.

• **Step 2:** Now make a loop with the two pieces and pass the end of the leader and the entire tippet through the loop.

≋

The four steps of tying the Double Surgeon's Knot.

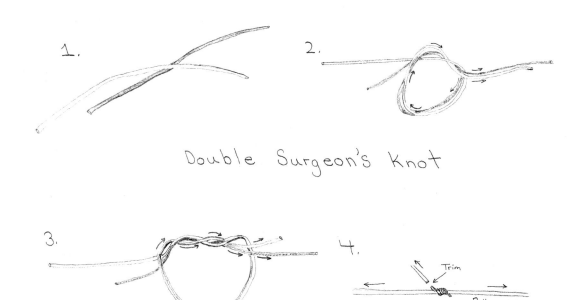

• Step 3: Now pass the same two pieces through the loop one more time. Then wet the knot with some spit. The spit will keep the line from weakening or breaking from the friction created when the knot is tightened.

• Step 4: Pull all four ends at the same time to start to tighten the knot. Finish tightening the knot by pulling the two short ends. Then trim the two tag ends (the short ends) close to the knot.

◉ ◉ ◉

Let's learn how to tie our fly onto the tippet with a Clinch Knot. This is an easy knot that works really well.

• Step 1: Put the tippet through the eye of the hook. Place about 6 inches through the hook eye and then lay it side by side with the long piece of tippet.

• Step 2: Wrap the short end around the long piece of tippet 4 to 6 times and then place the short end through the small opening in front of the hook eye.

• **Step 3:** Wet the line with some spit and then slowly pull on the long piece of tippet. Do not pull on the short end of the tippet or the knot will not tighten and will not be strong.

• **Step 4:** Once the knot is tightened, then trim the short end close to the knot. Now you are ready to start fishing!

The four steps of tying the Clinch Knot.

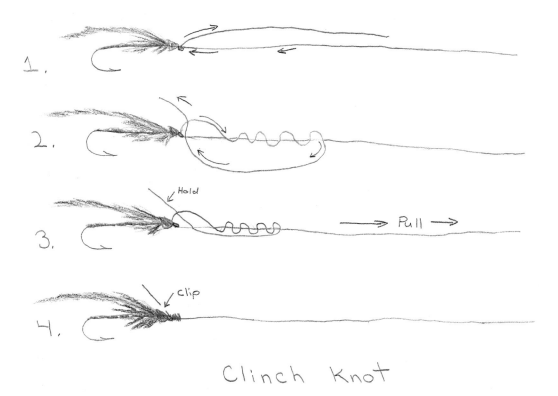

1.

2.

3.

Hold

Pull →

4.

clip

Clinch Knot

Flyfishing Techniques and Methods

There are many different methods and techniques for flyfishing that can be used to catch fish. We need to understand that fishing in rivers or moving water uses different techniques than if we are fishing in lakes or still water. In rivers, the bugs and insects float or drift in the water's currents. In lakes, the bugs and insects swim in the water to move around. The small minnows, leeches, and crayfish will swim in both rivers and lakes.

So when we fish in rivers we usually want our flies to drift like the natural insects so that the fish will be fooled. This is called a *drag-free drift*. We can fish flies on the surface, which is called *dry-fly fishing*; or we can fish flies below the surface, which is called *wet-fly fishing*, or *nymph fishing*. When we are stripping a fly (pulling line in with our non-casting hand once the fly has been cast into the water) to make it look like a small minnow or baitfish, this is called *streamer fishing*. Now let's learn how to use some of these different methods.

Dry-fly Fishing

Dry flies usually work best when there is a hatch. A hatch is when the bugs that live in the water or in the rocks and vegetation on the bottom of a lake or stream swim to the top of the water and become flying insects. When this happens, you will

A hatch is when the bugs swim to the top of the water and become flying insects.

usually see fish eating the bugs on top of the water, which is called *rising*. When dry-fly fishing on rivers, you will cast your fly above (upstream from) where the fish is rising and let the current carry the fly down to the fish. If you have matched the bug with the right kind of fly, you might fool the fish. It is important to let your fly drift to the fish like the natural bug. If it is dragging or skating on the surface, they may not eat your fly.

When fishing dry flies in a lake or pond, you try to cast the fly to a fish that has risen to a real bug and let it sit there on the surface waiting for the fish to swim up to it and eat it. Some insects do skitter on the surface like caddisflies, so you can cast your fly and strip line (pulling line in with your non-casting hand once the fly has been cast onto the water) to make your fly skitter like the real bug.

Once fish have been rising for bugs on the surface for some time, they will sometimes look up for food even when there is not a hatch going on. Fish will eat bugs like grasshoppers, crickets, beetles, and ants from the surface of the water during the summer months. This is a good time to fish with attractor dry flies. What are attractor dry flies you might ask? They are flies that do not look like any real bug and sometimes have bright colors or sparkly stuff on them to attract the fish.

Nymph Fishing

Any insect that lives in the water is called a nymph. This includes bugs like stoneflies, caddisflies, mayflies, dragonflies, damselflies, and midges. In a river or stream the real nymphs live down in the rocks, mud, and plants. Sometimes, the bugs get washed off the rocks and plants by the water current. When this happens, they drift along in the water where the fish can eat them. Also, when it is time for them to hatch, the nymph swims to the surface and the adult flying insect hatches out of the nymph.

The nymph flies usually need to be fished down close to the bottom. To do this we use flies with weight in them or with a metal bead on the front of them. We also add small sinkers called *split shot* onto our leader to help get them down near the bottom. Since we cannot see the fish eating our fly when it is down deep in the water, we use a strike indicator (bobber) so that we can tell when the fish has eaten our fly.

The way we use a strike indicator is to place it about two times the depth of the water above our fly (if the water we are fishing in is 3 feet deep, the strike indicator is placed on the leader 6 feet above the fly). The split shot is placed on the leader about 18″–24″ above our fly. We cast our nymph fishing set-up upstream into the current where we think there might be fish. It is best to make fairly short casts so you have good control of your line and the drift of your fly. The split shot will pull the fly down into the water as it is drifting along in the current. It is very important to make sure the strike indicator is

Nymph fishing set-up.

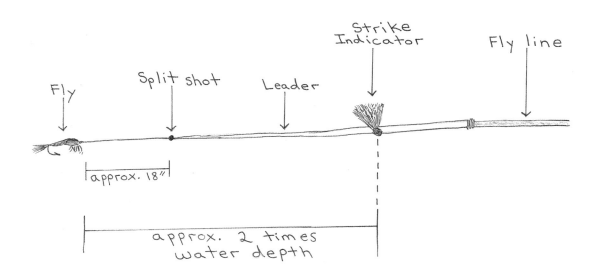

not dragging on the surface (if it is dragging it will look like a small motor boat leaving a wake behind it) because that means your nymph is also dragging and does not look like the real bugs drifting in the current.

If the strike indicator moves even the smallest amount, set the hook.

When the strike indictor moves slightly, bounces up and down slightly, or is pulled down under the water, it usually means a fish. But if it is not a fish, then it means your fly or split shot is probably in some weeds or touching a rock on the bottom of the river. You really have to pay attention to your strike indicator to make sure you do not miss any strikes. If the strike indicator moves even the smallest amount, set the hook. You set the hook by lifting the tip of your rod with a quick movement. Be careful not to set the hook too hard or you might break the leader and lose the fish. You will get better the more you practice. You will be surprised how gently the fish will eat your nymph fly.

When the strike indicator gets downstream at the end of your line, it will start to drag. That means it is time to cast back upstream to start a new drag-free drift with the fly. Sometimes, you might get a strike right at the end of your drift because your fly will start to rise to the surface as it is dragging. It looks like a bug swimming up to the surface to hatch.

Sometimes you may be able to see the fish you are casting to in a river if the water is very clear. This is called *sight nymphing*. When we sight fish, we pick a fish and cast our nymphing rig above the fish to allow it to sink to the depth the fish is at. Then the fun part is watching the fish to see if he eats that fly. There are times when you can actually see your fly and see the fish open its mouth to eat it. That is awesome when it happens! Sight nymphing is almost as much fun as watching a fish rise to a dry fly.

In lakes and ponds we can use split shot to help our nymphs sink or we can use a sinking fly line to help pull the fly down deep into the water. Usually we fish nymphs in lakes and ponds around structure because that is where the real bugs are living. Remember, in lakes and ponds the nymphs are not drifting but are crawling and swimming. So when we cast our line out, we let it sink and then we strip the fly line back into us with our non-casting hand to make it look like our nymph is swimming.

Streamer Fishing

Streamers are a type of fly that are supposed to look like small fish that trout, bass, pike, musky, crappie, and other fish like to eat. When we fish streamers in rivers or lakes we will usually cast them out and strip in the fly line to make them look like they are swimming.

Streamers are a type of fly that are supposed to look like small fish that other fish like to eat.

In rivers and streams I prefer to use a floating fly line and a leader that is about six to seven feet long. Some streamer flies have a bead head or cone on the front of them to help them sink. Others have weight under the body to help them sink. Remember you can always put split shot on your leader to help sink the fly. I like to fish streamers upstream, across stream, and downstream.

First, make your cast, and then let the fly sink for a couple of seconds. Then start to strip the line. It is a good idea to vary the type of stripping patterns to find out what the fish like that particular day. You may strip the fly with short fast strips or maybe long slow strips and even mixing it up with fast and slow strips on each cast. It is super duper important that you do not stop stripping the fly when you can see a fish following it.

Just imagine that you are a small minnow living in a river. You are just hanging out near the bank eating small bugs floating by in the current. Then you decide you are going to check out a new place downstream behind the next rock. So you start to cruise downstream when all of a sudden a large

Flyfishing is about learning
how to hook fish, fight fish, land fish,
and release fish properly
so you can catch them again.

trout is coming up behind you, very fast, with its mouth wide open. Do you just stop and let the big bad trout eat you or do you swim faster to try and get away? The right answer is that you probably would swim faster trying to get away. Use this as an example of how to fish your streamer fly if you see a fish following it. It probably does not look natural when a trout or other predator fish is chasing a minnow and it just stops. You may even want to strip your streamer fly faster when you see a trout following it.

Here is a Yellow Perch that ate my streamer fly.

6

Fish Food

As we have learned earlier in the book, the flies we use are usually supposed to look like some type of food that fish eat. It could be bugs that live in the water, or bugs that live out of the water but fall into the water. Other creatures like minnows, crayfish, snails, leeches, shrimp, frogs, and even mice are things that fish will eat.

Bugs That Live in the Water

There are many types of bugs that live in the water. Caddisflies, mayflies, midges, and stoneflies are some of the most common

Caddisflies, mayflies, midges, and stoneflies are some of the most common water insects you will see when you are out flyfishing.

water insects you will see when you are out flyfishing. Other water bugs include dragonflies, damselflies, and beetles. When the bugs are actually living in the water, they are called nymphs. At some point the nymph will swim to the surface or crawl out of the water onto the bank, a rock, or stick and hatch into a flying insect. We use dry flies to imitate the flying adult bugs. Remember nymphs sink and are fished underwater, and dry flies float and are fished on the surface of the water.

There are also many different types of aquatic bugs found in lakes and ponds. Midges, mayflies, and caddisflies can be found in lakes and ponds but there are also dragonflies and damselflies. Aquatic beetles and aquatic worms are also in many lakes and ponds.

Some hatches can have millions of bugs, and the fish will be very excited about eating, but can be very picky about the type of bug they are eating. So, we try to match the bugs that are hatching as closely as possible with our flies. If there are stoneflies hatching, we will probably not have very good luck if we fished a fly that looked like a midge. A better choice would be to fish a stonefly nymph or stonefly dry fly if we see fish rising on the surface. This is called *matching the hatch*. Most aquatic

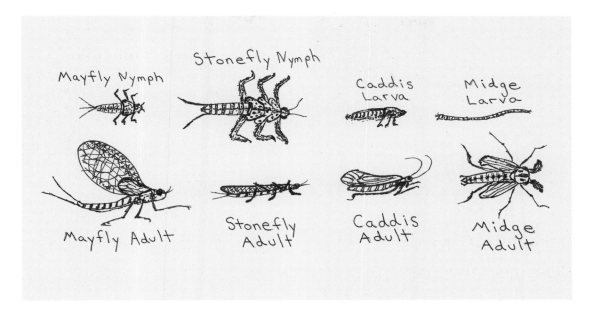

bugs only live for a very short time as a flying insect out of the water. There are always nymphs in the water so most trout, bass, and panfish do most of their feeding underwater on the nymphs and only a small amount of feeding on the surface unless there are hatches.

Bugs That Live out of the Water

The bugs that live out of the water but fall into the water, or are blown into the water by the wind, are called terrestrial insects. Terrestrial insects include grasshoppers, ants, beetles, crickets, and even things like ladybugs and moths. Trout, bass, and panfish really like to eat

The bugs that live out of the water but fall into the water, or are blown into the water, are called terrestrial insects.

LEFT: **Grasshopper** RIGHT: **Beetle**

terrestrial insects. Usually terrestrial insects float so we will use dry flies to match them. Since these bugs are usually only around during the warmer months they are not flies we need to have in our fly boxes during the winter time.

Terrestrial bugs can be blown by the wind out of the grass and bushes by a lake or stream and into the water. They can also be washed into the water from the rain. This often happens to ants on the edge of the water during a heavy rainstorm. When we walk around the edge of a lake or next to the bank of a river, we might even spook a grasshopper and they will jump right into the water and become food for the fish. There are many different flies which look like terrestrial insects (grasshoppers, ants, beetles and crickets) that we can use to catch fish.

Other Fish Foods

Fish like to eat a lot of different things and will usually eat living things that are found in or around the water they live in. Trout and bass will eat leeches, crayfish, snails, freshwater shrimp, frogs, and even mice!

Types of Artificial Flies

We have already learned that there are many types of artificial flies used to fool and catch fish. There are four primary types of flies. In this section we will learn about these different types and when we would usually fish them. Each type of fly—dry flies, nymphs, wet flies, and streamers—come in many different patterns. Patterns are specific flies based on their color or the certain list of materials used to make them. Fly patterns are like recipes you would use to cook a meal. An example would be a mayfly adult pattern, it could be a Blue Winged Olive or a Green Drake or a Pale Morning Dun. They all look like mayflies but use different materials and different colors that make them specific.

Dry Flies

Dry flies are flies that float on the surface of the water. Dry flies can be used to match a specific flying insect or an insect that floats on the water like a grasshopper. Other dry flies are called attractor dry flies. They do not look like any certain bug and usually have some bright colors or flashy material on them.

We fish dry flies when we see fish rising and eating food that floats. Attractor flies can be fished even when we do not see a hatch. Fish will look at the surface of the water if they get used to seeing bugs on the surface. We can use attractor flies to

Different kinds of dry flies.

try and lure them to the surface to eat our fly. Fishing dry flies is a lot of fun because you can see the fish eat your fly.

Nymphs

Nymphs are flies that sink and are used to match specific bugs that live in the water like stoneflies, caddisflies, and damselflies, just to name a few. There are also nymph fly patterns that are attractor flies. They usually do not look like a specific bug. Some have metal beads on the front of them to help them sink or flashy material on them to make them more visible in discolored water.

Since the bugs that live in the water are always available for the fish to eat, fish do most of their feeding on nymphs. We can fish nymphs all year long in the rivers and streams or in lakes before any hatches start. Usually, you do not see your nymphs down in the water because the split shot on your leader takes them down near the bottom where the real bugs live. If the water is very clear you can sometimes see your flies and the fish you are casting to. This is called *sight nymphing.*

Wet Flies

Traditional wet flies are flies that sink, but many of them do not look like any type of bug. Most of them have bright colors and

Different kinds of nymphs.

flashy material. They are pretty much attractor flies that sink. They can be fished with split shot on the leader to help them sink, using a drag-free drift. They can also be fished by casting across the river's current and allowed to swing or drag back across the current like you might fish a streamer. The fish will usually eat them while they are swinging. This can be some exciting fishing because the strikes are sometimes explosive when the fish eats the fly.

Streamers

Streamers are flies that sink. We use them to match minnows or other small fish like baby trout or baby bluegill. Streamers are

LEFT: **Different kinds of wet flies.** RIGHT: **Different kinds of streamers.**

very fun to fish because you cast them out and strip your line back in to make them swim like a small fish. When trout and bass eat streamers, they really attack them. Sometimes you can see the fish following your streamer if the water is really clear or if you are fishing from a boat. Streamer flies can be fished all year round because there are always small fish in the water. Streamers are a good fly type to fish places you have never been before since you can fish through different areas quickly with a streamer. This is because you are stripping the fly and fishing the water effectively with many casts in a short amount of time.

Here is a carp that ate my nymph while I was fishing for panfish.

7

Flyfishing Is More Than Catching Fish

Flyfishing is an adventure that allows boys and girls like you to do many different things. I have been very lucky to have the opportunity to learn new things and visit many new places because of flyfishing. I have been able to meet a lot of neat people that flyfish, people that tie flies, people that do fish artwork, people that write books and articles about flyfishing, and people that have been so willing to teach me about different parts

Flyfishing is an adventure

> *Fly tying is an art form just like flyfishing, but you are making something.*

of flyfishing. Because of flyfishing I have been able to learn about fish, about bugs, about speaking in front of a group of people, about photography, about drawing and painting fish, and even about writing a book.

One fun thing to learn is fly tying. Fly tying is an art form just like flyfishing, but you are making something. There are neat materials like feathers, fur, flashy stuff, beads, hooks, and thread that we get to use to create a fly pattern. There are some tools that you need to tie flies, such as a vise to hold the hook, a bobbin that holds the fly tying thread, and a half-hitch or whip finish tool to help you tie the knot in the thread when you are finished tying the fly. Fly tying lets you invent new flies and be creative. Some people that tie flies do not even fish. They

Tyler tying flies.

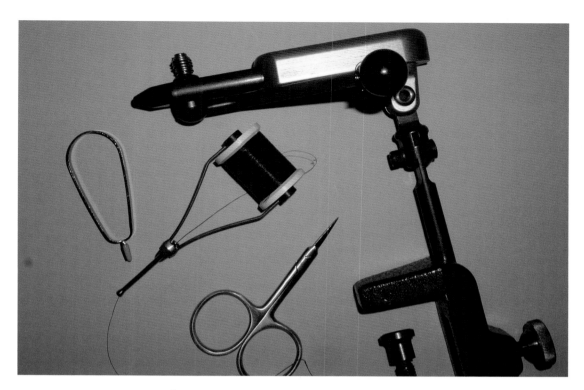

TOP: **Fly tying tools.** BELOW: **Fly tying materials.**

Tyler inspecting bugs found on the rocks of the river.

do it because they like the art form. It is very rewarding to catch fish on flies that you tied yourself. It is pretty neat to learn about all of the different fly tying materials.

I got to tour Whiting Farms; they are a company that raises chickens for fly tying feathers. They sell their feathers all over the world. I got to see how they hatch the eggs and grow the chickens so we can use them to tie our flies. It was an honor for me that they asked me to become their youngest pro team member. I have a special shirt they sent me with my name on it that I wear when I do my fly tying demonstrations at shows and at schools.

Learning about the bugs and different things that fish eat is also exciting. Studying bugs is called entomology. This is like a science class. You can go out and turn over the rocks in a river or stream, or dig through the weeds in a lake with your hands, to

Sculpins are fish that live on the bottom of some rivers and trout love to eat them.

discover the different types of bugs living in the water you are fishing in. This will help make you a better flyfisher. There are books that teach you about different bugs and that can also help you figure out what kind of bugs you have found. Sometimes we put the bugs in glass jars with water to watch them. My dad even helped me put up an aquarium in our house with bugs and some small fish called sculpins. Sculpins are fish that live on the bottom of some rivers and trout love to eat them.

You can meet neat people from all over the world who also like to flyfish. In Japan I have a friend named Masa Katsumata. He taught me about fishing with really tiny flies for the different kinds of trout that live in Japan. He has also invited my dad and me to come and fish with him in Japan. I can't wait for that trip! I also have a friend who lives in Denmark. His name is Jens Pilgaard, and he taught me how to tie flies without using a vise to hold the hook but by using just your fingers—like people used to do to tie flies a long time ago. Jens even makes some of his own hooks that he uses to tie flies on. That's cool!

You can meet neat people from all over the world who also like to flyfish.

LEFT: **Tyler and Masa fishing on the Lake Fork of the Gunnison River.**
RIGHT: **Tyler and Jens at the Flyfishing show, Somerset, New Jersey.**

My friend Jeff Currier who lives in Idaho, is an awesome fish artist. He taught me how to sketch fish while we were at a flyfishing show at the University of Wyoming. Now I spend a lot of time drawing fish with colored pencils and painting fish with watercolors. This is a fun thing to do when we are riding in the car to go fishing or when we are riding home. You can

My friend Yugi and I tying flies while I was in Japan.

Jeff Currier with a carp caught
in Wyoming.

with my dad. There are too
many fly tiers to mention all
of them who have helped
with my fly tying and have
generously given me one of
their flies. Some of these
people I only get to see once

draw a picture of one of the
fish you caught that day. I
like art and I was able to draw
some of the fish in this book.

I like to collect different
flies from different fly tiers
from all over the world when
I meet them at flyfishing or
fly tying shows that I go to

Tyler with fly tier Harrison Steeves
of Virginia.

Tyler with Martin Westbeek of the Netherlands.

a year, and it is fun to talk to them about the fishing they have been doing or the flies they have been tying.

Our family friends Pat and Carol Oglesby, who live in Grand Junction, Colorado, are some of my favorite fishing buddies. We've spent a lot of time fishing together. They have taught me about the outdoors, wildlife, photography, and the history of the Gunnison River, which is my favorite river to fish in Colorado. They also got me my first pair of high-tech waders.

Tyler with Pat and Carol Oglesby eating lunch on the river.

One of the coolest things I like about flyfishing is that I get to travel to new places and see some really cool things when we go fishing. Sometimes we ride in the car and I can watch out the window for wildlife like deer, elk, eagles, and even bears. I like road trips in the car. My dad took me to Rocky Mountain National Park to fish for greenback cutthroat trout. It was a long ride from our house, but it was worth it to catch these awesome trout. Other times we fly in an airplane to go fishing or to go to a sportsman's show where I will be tying flies or

Black bear on the Innoko River, Alaska.

A big elk in Rocky Mountain National Park.

giving presentations about flyfishing. It was a lot of fun when I flew in different airplanes to go to Alaska. That is a trip I will never forget. I got to see moose, bears, and eagles while I was there. Oh yeah, I did catch a few fish too!

I think the best thing about flyfishing is the time I get to spend with my family enjoying the outdoors. I get to help my little sisters learn about all the different things we just talked about. Sometimes I help my mom land a fish she has hooked. Even if we fish just a little bit or do not even catch a single fish, it is still a great time. Every flyfisher has their own idea of why they flyfish. For me it is much more than just catching fish—it is about the adventure. Are you ready? **Now let's start your flyfishing adventure!**

I think the best thing about flyfishing is the time I get to spend with my family.

Tyler Befus

Tyler Befus has been flyfishing with his parents since he was old enough to go along in a child backpack. He started fly casting and fly tying at the age of three and landed his first fly-caught trout on his own shortly before his third birthday. He is the youngest member of the Whiting Farms, Rio Products, and Ross Reels pro staff teams and is a fly designer for Umpqua Feather Merchants. Tyler has been a featured fly tier at the Western Colorado Fly Fishing Exposition in Grand Junction, Colorado, for six years, the Blac ose, Colorado, as well as the Fly Fishi

Additional competitions and has placed among ig fish artist doing his work with col to his determination, angling skills, and passion for the sport of flyfishing, he currently holds two International Gamefish Association (IGFA) Junior World Records.

Recently, he started delivering slide presentations about youth and flyfishing for local schools and Trout Unlimited groups in Colorado and will be a featured speaker at the flyfishing shows in Denver, Colorado, and Somerset, New Jersey. He is committed to introducing other kids to the sport of flyfishing so they too can enjoy this great adventure. Tyler lives in Montrose, Colorado, with his parents and two sisters.